Comprehension 1: The Wizard of Oz

The houses of the city were all made of transparent that one could look through the walls as easily as through a window. Dorothy saw, underneath the roof on which she stood, several rooms used for rest chambers, and even thought she could make out a number of queer forms huddled into the corners of these rooms.

The roof beside them had a great hole smashed through it, and pieces of glass were lying scattered in every direction. A nearby steeple had been broken off short and the fragments lay heaped beside it. Other buildings were cracked in places or had corners chipped off from them; but they must have been very beautiful before these accidents had happened to mar their perfection. The rainbow tints from the coloured suns fell upon the glass city softly and gave to the buildings many delicate, shifting hues which were very pretty to see.

But not a sound had broken the stillness since the strangers had arrived, except that of their own voices. They began to wonder if there were no people to inhabit this magnificent city of the inner world.

Suddenly a man appeared through a hole in the roof next to the one they were on and stepped into plain view. He was not a very large man, but was well formed and had a beautiful face — serene as the face of a fine portrait. His clothing fitted his form snugly and was gorgeously coloured in brilliant shades of green, which varied as the sunbeams touched them but was not wholly influenced by the solar rays.

The man had taken a step or two across the glass roof before he noticed the presence of the strangers; but then he stopped abruptly. There was no expression of either fear or surprise upon his tranquil face, yet he must have been both astonished and afraid; for after his eyes had rested upon the ungainly form of the horse for a moment he walked rapidly to the furthest edge of the roof, his head turned back over his shoulder to gaze at the strange animal.

"Look out!" cried Dorothy, who noticed that the beautiful man did not look where he was going; "be careful, or you'll fall off!"

But he paid no attention to her warning. He reached the edge of the tall roof, stepped one foot out into the air, and walked into space as calmly as if he were on firm ground.

The girl, greatly astonished, ran to lean over the edge of the roof, and saw the man walking rapidly through the air toward the ground. Soon he reached the street and disappeared through a glass doorway into one of the glass buildings.

"How strange!" she exclaimed, drawing a long breath.

"Yes; but it's lots of fun, if it IS strange," remarked the small voice of the kitten, and Dorothy turned to find her pet walking in the air a foot or so away from the edge of the roof.

"Come back, Eureka!" she called, in distress, "you'll certainly be killed."

"I have nine lives," said the kitten, purring softly as it walked around in a circle and then came back to the roof; "but I can't lose even one of them by falling in this country, because I really couldn't manage to fall if I wanted to."

Mark your answers on the answer sheet.

1. The walls of the houses in the city were made from:

    A) Stone
    B) Glass
    C) Concrete
    D) Plastic

2. Dorothy could see many rooms underneath the roof. What were they?

    A) Kitchens
    B) Classrooms
    C) Bedrooms
    D) Nurseries

3. What made the city's buildings very pretty to see?

    A) Their shade
    B) Their height
    C) Their structure
    D) The doors

4. In the phrase 'had happened to mar their perfection', what does the word 'mar' mean?

    A) accidental
    B) ruin
    C) light
    D) question

5. In the phrase 'shifting hues which were very pretty to see', what does the word 'hue' mean?

    A) thought
    B) colour
    C) dull
    D) sunlight

6. 'They began to wonder if there were no people to inhabit magnificent city of the inner world.' Why did they think this?

    A) they couldn't hear any voices
    B) the colours were out of this world
    C) it was dark and dull
    D) they couldn't see anything

7. What was the man who appeared like?

    A) Huge
    B) Calm and collected
    C) Angry
    D) Upset

8. Why do you think the man ignored Dorothy?

    A) He could not hear her
    B) He found Dorothy annoying
    C) He could not see her
    D) He knew he wouldn't fall

9. Why is Dorothy afraid that Eureka will be severely hurt?
    A) She is afraid he will fall
    B) She thinks the man will take Eureka
    C) She thinks a predator will eat her
    D) She is afraid he will run away

magical minds+

Answer Sheet: Comprehension 1

Mark your answers with a pencil like this:

~~[A]~~

1	[A]	[B]	[C]	[D]
2	[A]	[B]	[C]	[D]
3	[A]	[B]	[C]	[D]
4	[A]	[B]	[C]	[D]
5	[A]	[B]	[C]	[D]
6	[A]	[B]	[C]	[D]
7	[A]	[B]	[C]	[D]
8	[A]	[B]	[C]	[D]
9	[A]	[B]	[C]	[D]

Mark: [   ] / 9

Comprehension 2: Egyptian Pyramids

The pyramids that we see in Egypt today continue to be 'Wonders of the World'. They were built thousands of years ago and yet they still stand. The ancient Egyptians created the pyramids as burial tombs to honour their pharaohs and since they believe them to be both man and god, they made the pyramids in a grand style.

It's believed that the original burial tombs for pharaohs and high ranking officials were flat monuments called 'mastabas'. Over the years, each new burial tomb would have another smaller layer added to the top until they began to look like steps. The building of pyramids reached its height in the Old Kingdom time, between the Fourth and Sixth Dynasties. There are over 70 pyramids near the Nile River. It is thought that the first smooth sided pyramid was built between the years of 2680 to 2560 BC for the pharaoh Snefru. Archeological excavations have found that unlike what most people might think, the pyramids were not built by slaves, but were Egyptians that lived in the area. They have found living areas that appear to be for the labourers and their families in an almost community style. The villages seem to be set up with shops, houses, butcher shops and even bakeries for the thousands of loaves of bread that was needed to feed the workers.

There was a lot of planning that went into building a pyramid. Because of the weight, the location had to be on firm rock because building on sand would cause it to collapse. Specific measurements had to be made on the base size width and length. This was one of the most important decisions because it they were off, the pyramid would fall. Rock was cut out from quarries that were often quite a distance and carried on boats on the River Nile to the pyramid location. There were millions of pieces of rock that had to be just the right size to fit in place.

Egyptologists are not really sure how the ancient Egyptians managed to get the heavy rock, often weighing many tons up to build the pyramids. Some think that they used ramps, while others think that they may have used sand to release and balance. There are many people throughout the world today that have tried to build smaller pyramids to figure out exactly how it was done.

One of the things that everyone notices about the pyramids of Egypt is that they are incredibly large. The smallest of the Giza pyramids is over 200 feet high. The pyramid built by the pharaoh Khufu was originally 480 feet high and is made up of over 2.3 million stone blocks. Each of the blocks weighs about 5,000 lbs and had to be cut to the right size, brought to the pyramid and put in place by hand. The engineers of ancient Egypt were familiar with the difficult mathematics that were involved in creating a structure of such size. The ancient Egyptian engineers planned the blocks so that there were inner chambers and tunnels. It was thought that the pyramid chambers were for the burial of the pharaohs. Some of the huge stone burial sarcophagus have been found inside the pyramids but never any of the mummies or anything that would have been buried with the pharaoh.

Once a pyramid was completed, it had armed guards to try to protect it from tomb raiders. The tombs were raided on such a regular basis that it is thought that the secrets were told to others by the builders. If anyone was caught raiding a pharaoh's tomb, it was an instance death sentence.

The pyramids that we see today have crumbled quite a bit and don't look at all like they would have upon completion. Once all of the stones were in place, the entire pyramid was covered in white limestone and the top or cap of the pyramid would have been tipped in gold. In the bright Egyptian sunshine, the white and the gold would have gleamed brightly.

Mark your answers on the answer sheet.

1. What purpose did the Ancient Egyptians build pyramids for?

   A) To hide
   B) As a monument for the people
   C) Everybody was buried in pyramids
   D) Burial tombs to honour their Pharaohs

2. Why were the Pyramids built so grandly?

   A) Because they needed to be big to fit in everyone
   B) Pharaohs were believed to be like man and God
   C) They were not built grandly
   D) Because a Pharaoh demanded it

3. What were the original burial tombs for pharaohs and high ranking officials called?

   A) Mastabas
   B) Pyramids
   C) Tombs
   D) The secret room

4. Approximately, how many pyramids are near the river Nile?

   A) It is not known
   B) 70
   C) 100
   D) 30

5. Who is it thought the first smooth-sided pyramid was built for?

      A) Snefru
      B) Cleopatra
      C) Khufu
      D) Teti

6. Who is thought to have built the pyramids?

      A) Slaves
      B) Pharaohs
      C) Egyptians who lived in the area
      D) Maids

7. Where did pyramids have to be built?

      A) Firm stone
      B) Grass
      C) Anywhere where there was space
      D) Sand

8. Pyramids had armed guards to protect them from:

      A) Crumbling
      B) To make sure nobody would destroy the pyramids
      C) Tomb-raiders
      D) To stop them from falling

9. Once all of the stones were in place, sometimes the pyramid would be covered with:
    A) White limestone
    B) Marble

C) Thin stone

D) Sand

Answer Sheet: Comprehension 2

Mark your answers with a pencil like this:

[A]

1	[A]	[B]	[C]	[D]
2	[A]	[B]	[C]	[D]
3	[A]	[B]	[C]	[D]
4	[A]	[B]	[C]	[D]
5	[A]	[B]	[C]	[D]
6	[A]	[B]	[C]	[D]
7	[A]	[B]	[C]	[D]
8	[A]	[B]	[C]	[D]
9	[A]	[B]	[C]	[D]

Mark: ☐ / 9

Comprehension 3: The Strange Case of Dr Jekyll and Mr Hyde

Mr. Utterson the lawyer was a man of a rugged countenance that was never lighted by a smile; cold, scanty and embarrassed in discourse; backward in sentiment; lean, long, dusty, dreary and yet somehow lovable.

At friendly meetings, and when the wine was to his taste, something eminently human beaconed from his eye; something indeed which never found its way into his talk, but which spoke not only in these silent symbols of the after-dinner face, but more often and loudly in the acts of his life. He was austere with himself; drank gin when he was alone, to mortify a taste for vintages; and though he enjoyed the theatre, had not crossed the doors of one for twenty years. But he had an approved tolerance for others; sometimes wondering, almost with envy, at the high pressure of spirits involved in their misdeeds; and in any extremity inclined to help rather than to reprove. "I incline to Cain's heresy," he used to say quaintly: "I let my brother go to the devil in his own way." In this character, it was frequently his fortune to be the last reputable acquaintance and the last good influence in the lives of downgoing men. And to such as these, so long as they came about his

chambers, he never marked a shade of change in his demeanour.

No doubt the feat was easy to Mr. Utterson; for he was undemonstrative at the best, and even his friendship seemed to be founded in a similar catholicity of good-nature. It is the mark of a modest man to accept his friendly circle ready-made from the hands of opportunity; and that was the lawyer's way. His friends were those of his own blood or those whom he had known the longest; his affections, like ivy, were the growth of time, they implied no aptness in the object. Hence, no doubt the bond that united him to Mr. Richard Enfield, his distant kinsman, the well-known man about town. It was a nut to crack for many, what these

two could see in each other, or what subject they could find in common. It was reported by those who encountered them in their

Sunday walks, that they said nothing, looked singularly dull and would hail with obvious relief the appearance of a friend. For all that, the two men put the greatest store by these excursions, counted them the chief jewel of each week, and not only set aside occasions of pleasure, but even resisted the calls of business, that they might enjoy them uninterrupted.

Mark your answers on the answer sheet.

1. What was Mr Utterson's occupation?

   A) A teacher
   B) A lawyer
   C) He had no job
   D) An engineer

2. What type of person is Mr Utterson described as?

   A) Morose and boring
   B) Friendly
   C) Curt and abrupt
   D) Angry

3. 'He was austere with himself.' What does 'austere' mean?
   A) Friendly
   B) Egoistic
   C) Selfish
   D) Harsh

4. When did Mr Utterson last go to the theatre?

    A) Last year
    B) 2 days ago
    C) 20 years ago
    D) He had never been-he hated theatres.

5. What does the phrase 'he never marked a shade of change in his demeanour' mean?

    A) He was never mean
    B) His manner always stayed the same
    C) His personality kept on changing
    D) He was very kind

6. Most of Utterson's friends were:

    A) Friends from work
    B) His family
    C) He had no friends
    D) His servants

7. Why did people find it strange that Utterson and Enfield were friends?

    A) They hated each other in school
    B) Their families were rivals
    C) They were family
    D) Enfield was very lively, and Utterson was gloomy

8. What did Utterson and Enfield do on Sundays?

    A) They went on a walk together

B) They went to the library and read

C) They went to Dr Jekyll's house

D) Nothing- they only met occasionally

9. They 'counted them the chief jewel of each week', what does this mean?

　　A) Every week they found a jewel.

　　B) They hated the trip.

　　C) Their trip was very important each week.

　　D) They did the trip just because they were cousins.

Answer Sheet: Comprehension 3

Mark your answers with a pencil like this:

　　[A]

1	[A]	[B]	[C]	[D]
2	[A]	[B]	[C]	[D]
3	[A]	[B]	[C]	[D]
4	[A]	[B]	[C]	[D]
5	[A]	[B]	[C]	[D]
6	[A]	[B]	[C]	[D]
7	[A]	[B]	[C]	[D]
8	[A]	[B]	[C]	[D]
9	[A]	[B]	[C]	[D]

Mark: ☐ / 9

Comprehension 4: Florence Nightingale

Florence Nightingale went to the Crimean War to nurse wounded soldiers. She and her nurses saved many lives.

Florence was born in 1820. This was ten years before Britain had its first steam passenger railway. She lived through the long reign of Queen Victoria. She died in 1910, after the age of electricity, cars and planes began.

Florence Nightingale made hospitals cleaner places. She showed that trained nurses and clean hospitals helped sick people get better. She was the founder of modern nursing.

Florence's father was William Nightingale, a rich banker. William and his wife Fanny went to Italy after they married in 1818, where they stayed. Florence was born in Italy on 12th May. She was named after the city of her birth. Florence had an older sister, Frances Parthenope. The girls had lessons from their father. Florence was clever, and liked learning about events of the past and numbers.

The Nightingales had a winter home in Hampshire and a summer home in Derbyshire. They had servants.

In Victorian Britain, poor women worked as servants or in factories. Rich girls like Florence were expected to marry and look after a home, perhaps doing charity work.

Florence was very religious. From the age of sixteen, she believed God wanted her to do important work. When she was twenty-two, a young writer asked her to marry him. After seven years making up her mind, Florence said no.

Florence wanted to be a nurse- but when she told her parents, they were shocked. Hospitals at this time were dirty and horrible, and it wasn't seen as something respectable.

Mark your answers on the answer sheet

1. What war did Florence Nightingale save many lives in?

    A) WW1
    B) WW2
    C) Civil War
    D) Crimean War

2. When did Britain have its first steam passenger railway?

    A) 1820
    B) 1810
    C) 1830
    D) 1840

3. Who was the British Monarch in Nightingale's time?
    A) Queen Elizabeth
    B) Queen Victoria
    C) King James
    D) King Charles

4. What was the profession of her father?
    A) A doctor
    B) A lawyer
    C) A teacher
    D) A banker

5. Where was Florence born?

    A) Verona
    B) Venice
    C) Florence
    D) Paris

6. Who was Florence's teacher?

   A) Her father
   B) A governess
   C) Her mother
   D) Her grandmother

7. What subjects did Florence enjoy?

   A) History and English
   B) Geography and Maths
   C) Maths and History
   D) Art and Science

8. In the Victorian times, what were girls like Florence expected to do?

   A) Marry and do charity work
   B) Work in factories
   C) Be servants
   D) Have a respectable job

9. What were hospitals like in Victorian times?
   A) Very unclean and dirty
   B) Extremely clean
   C) It wasn't thought of
   D) Very good healthcare

Answer Sheet: Comprehension 4

Mark your answers with a pencil like this:
        [A]

1	[A]	[B]	[C]	[D]
2	[A]	[B]	[C]	[D]
3	[A]	[B]	[C]	[D]
4	[A]	[B]	[C]	[D]
5	[A]	[B]	[C]	[D]
6	[A]	[B]	[C]	[D]
7	[A]	[B]	[C]	[D]
8	[A]	[B]	[C]	[D]
9	[A]	[B]	[C]	[D]

Mark: ☐ / 9

Comprehension 5: What Katy Did

Katy's name was Katy Carr. She lived in the town of Burnet, which wasn't a very big town, but was growing as fast as it knew how. The house she lived in stood on the edge of the town. It was a large square house, white, with green blinds, and had a porch in front, over which roses and clematis made a thick bower. Four tall locust trees shaded the gravel path which led to the front gate. On one side of the house was an orchard; on the other side were wood piles and barns, and an ice-house. Behind was a kitchen garden sloping to the south; and behind that a pasture with a brook in it, and butternut trees, and four cows--two red ones, a yellow one with sharp horns tipped with tin, and a dear little white one named Daisy.

There were six of the Carr children--four girls and two boys. Katy, the oldest, was twelve years old; little Phil, the youngest, was four, and the rest fitted in between.

Dr. Carr, their Papa, was a dear, kind, busy man, who was away from home all day, and sometimes all night, too, taking care of sick people. The children hadn't any Mamma. She had died when Phil was a baby, four years before my story began. Katy could remember her pretty well; to the rest she was but a sad, sweet name, spoken on Sunday, and at prayer-times, or when Papa was especially gentle and solemn.

In place of this Mamma, whom they recollected so dimly, there was Aunt Izzie, Papa's sister, who came to take care of them when Mamma went away on that long journey, from which, for so many months, the little ones kept hoping she might return. Aunt Izzie was a small woman, sharp-faced and thin, rather old-looking, and very neat and particular about everything. She meant to be kind to the children, but they puzzled her much, because they were not a bit like herself when she was a child.

Aunt Izzie had been a gentle, tidy little thing, who loved to sit as

Curly Locks did, sewing long seams in the parlour, and to have her head patted by older people, and be told that she was a good girl; whereas Katy tore her dress every day, hated sewing, and didn't care a button about being called "good," while Clover and Elsie shied off like restless ponies when any one tried to pat their heads. It was very perplexing to Aunt Izzie, and she found it hard to quite forgive the children for being so "unaccountable," and so little like the good boys and girls in Sunday-school memoirs, who were the young people she liked best, and understood most about.

Then Dr. Carr was another person who worried her. He wished to have the children hardy and bold, and encouraged climbing and rough plays, in spite of the bumps and ragged clothes which resulted. In fact, there was just one half-hour of the day when Aunt Izzie was really satisfied about her charges, and that was the half-hour before breakfast, when she had made a law that they were all to sit in their little chairs and learn the Bible verse for the day. At this time she looked at them with pleased eyes, they were all so spick and span, with such nicely-brushed jackets and such neatly-combed hair. But the moment the bell rang her comfort was over. From that time on, they were what she called "not fit to be seen."

Mark your answer on the answer sheet?

1. Describe Katy's house.

    A) Square and white
    B) Green and rectangular
    C) Large and painted green
    D) She lived in a flat

2. What lay south of Katy's house?

    A) An ice house

B) An orchard

C) A vegetable/fruit garden

D) A wood

3. Who/what was Daisy?

A) A flower

B) A cow

C) Katy's sister

D) Katy's best friend

4. How many sisters did Katy have?

A) Two

B) Three

C) Four

D) None

5. How old was Katy's youngest brother?

A) Three

B) Four

C) Nine

D) Seven

6. Why was Katy's father often away from home?

A) He was sick in hospital

B) He had died

C) He was a doctor

D) He had a night shift at a shop

7. Who looked after the children?

    A) Their staff-member
    B) Their mother
    C) Their father's sister
    D) Their grandmother

8. Why did the children confuse Izzy?

    A) Because they always fought with eachother
    B) Because she hated them, and they hated her back
    C) They always tricked her and played pranks
    D) They were very different to her as a child

9. Izzy seems to be:

    A) Prim and proper
    B) Cantankerous
    C) Miserable
    D) Gullible

10. What did they do for half an hour before breakfast?

    A) Talk to each other
    B) Study the bible
    C) Do their homework
    D) Sing in a chorus

Answer Sheet: Comprehension 5

Mark your answers with a pencil like this:

[A]

1	[A]	[B]	[C]	[D]
2	[A]	[B]	[C]	[D]
3	[A]	[B]	[C]	[D]
4	[A]	[B]	[C]	[D]
5	[A]	[B]	[C]	[D]
6	[A]	[B]	[C]	[D]
7	[A]	[B]	[C]	[D]
8	[A]	[B]	[C]	[D]
9	[A]	[B]	[C]	[D]
10	[A]	[B]	[C]	[D]

Mark: ☐ / 10

Comprehension 6: Black Beauty

I was now beginning to grow handsome; my coat had grown fine and soft, and was bright black. I had one white foot and a pretty white star on my forehead. I was thought very handsome; my master would not sell me till I was four years old; he said lads ought not to work like men, and colts ought not to work like horses till they were quite grown up.

When I was four years old Squire Gordon came to look at me. He examined my eyes, my mouth, and my legs; he felt them all down; and then I had to walk and trot and gallop before him. He seemed to like me, and said, "When he has been well broken in he will do very well." My master said he would break me in himself, as he should not like me to be frightened or hurt, and he lost no time about it, for the next day he began.

Every one may not know what breaking in is, therefore I will describe it. It means to teach a horse to wear a saddle and bridle, and to carry on his back a man, woman or child; to go just the way they wish, and to go quietly. Besides this he has to learn to wear a collar, a crupper, and a breeching, and to stand still while they are put on; then to have a cart or a chaise fixed behind, so that he cannot walk or trot without dragging it after him; and he must go fast or slow, just as his driver wishes. He must never start at what he sees, nor speak to other horses, nor bite, nor kick, nor have any will of his own; but always do his master's will, even though he may be very tired or hungry; but the worst of all is, when his harness is once on, he may neither jump for joy nor lie down for weariness. So you see this breaking in is a great thing.

I had of course long been used to a halter and a headstall, and to be led about in the fields and lanes quietly, but now I was to have a bit and bridle; my master gave me some oats as usual, and after a good deal of coaxing he got the bit into my mouth, and the bridle fixed, but it was a nasty thing! Those who have never had a bit in their

mouths cannot think how bad it feels; a great piece of cold hard steel as thick as a man's finger to be pushed into one's mouth, between one's teeth, and over one's tongue, with the ends coming out at the corner of your mouth, and held fast there by straps over your head, under your throat, round your nose, and under your chin; so that no way in the world can you get rid of the nasty hard thing; it is very bad! yes, very bad! at least I thought so; but I knew my mother always wore one when she went out, and all horses did when they were grown up; and so, what with the nice oats, and what with my master's pats, kind words, and gentle ways, I got to wear my bit and bridle.

Next came the saddle, but that was not half so bad; my master put it on my back very gently, while old Daniel held my head; he then made the girths fast under my body, patting and talking to me all the time; then I had a few oats, then a little leading about; and this he did every day till I began to look for the oats and the saddle. At length, one morning, my master got on my back and rode me round the meadow on the soft grass. It certainly did feel queer; but I must say I felt rather proud to carry my master, and as he continued to ride me a little every day I soon became accustomed to it.

The next unpleasant business was putting on the iron shoes; that too was very hard at first. My master went with me to the smith's forge, to see that I was not hurt or got any fright. The blacksmith took my feet in his hand, one after the other, and cut away some of the hoof. It did not pain me, so I stood still on three legs till he had done them all. Then he took a piece of iron the shape of my foot, and clapped it on, and drove some nails through the shoe quite into my hoof, so that the shoe was firmly on. My feet felt very stiff and heavy, but in time I got used to it.

Mark your answers on the answer sheet.

1. What age would the master sell Black Beauty?

    A) Two
    B) Four
    C) Six months
    D) Six

2. What was the name of Black Beauty's master?

    A) Squire Ronald
    B) Master Donald
    C) Squire Gordon
    D) Unknown

3. 'Breaking in' seems to be a quite important event for a horse. What is it?

    A) Getting a horse ready for riding people
    B) Fitting on the horse shoe
    C) Learning how to walk
    D) Feeding the horse lots of food

4. What did Black Beauty usually eat?

    A) Grass
    B) Straw
    C) Apples
    D) Oats

5. How did he eventually get the 'bit' in his mouth?

    A) The master forced it his mouth
    B) He remembered his mother wearing it
    C) He liked the taste of it
    D) By eating seven apples

6. How did he feel when riding his master around the meadow?

    A) He detested it
    B) He loved it from the start
    C) Scary
    D) A bit strange

7. In the phrase 'I soon became accustomed to it', what does 'accustomed' mean?

    A) Used to
    B) Embarrassed
    C) Confused
    D) Angry

8. Where did Black Beauty go to get his shoes made?

    A) The stable
    B) The blacksmith
    C) The vet
    D) The meadow

9. Why did the horse's master go with him to get his shoes done?

A) To say goodbye
B) To leave him
C) To make sure Black Beauty didn't get hurt
D) He didn't go with him

Answer Sheet: Comprehension 6

Mark your answers with a pencil like this:
[A]

1	[A]	[B]	[C]	[D]
2	[A]	[B]	[C]	[D]
3	[A]	[B]	[C]	[D]
4	[A]	[B]	[C]	[D]
5	[A]	[B]	[C]	[D]
6	[A]	[B]	[C]	[D]
7	[A]	[B]	[C]	[D]
8	[A]	[B]	[C]	[D]
9	[A]	[B]	[C]	[D]

Mark: ☐ / 9

Comprehension 7: Pollyanna

In due time came the telegram announcing that Pollyanna would arrive in Beldingsville the next day, the twenty-fifth of June, at four o'clock. Miss Polly read the telegram, frowned, then climbed the stairs to the attic room. She still frowned as she looked about her.

 The room contained a small bed, neatly made, two straight-backed chairs, a washstand, a bureau--without any mirror--and a small table. There were no drapery curtains at the dormer windows, no pictures on the wall. All day the sun had been pouring down upon the roof, and the little room was like an oven for heat. As there were no screens, the windows had not been raised. A big fly was buzzing angrily at one of them now, up and down, up and down, trying to get out.

Miss Polly killed the fly, swept it through the window (raising the sash an inch for the purpose), straightened a chair, frowned again, and left the room.

"Nancy," she said a few minutes later, at the kitchen door, "I found a fly up-stairs in Miss Pollyanna's room. The window must have been raised at some time. I have ordered screens, but until they come I shall expect you to see that the windows remain closed. My niece will arrive tomorrow at four o'clock. I desire you to meet her at the station. Timothy will take the open buggy and drive you over. The telegram says 'light hair, red-checked gingham dress, and straw hat.' That is all I know, but I think it is sufficient for your purpose."

"Yes, ma'am; but--you--"

Miss Polly evidently read the pause aright, for she frowned and said crisply;
"No, I shall not go. It is not necessary that I should, I think. That is

all." And she turned away--Miss Polly's arrangements for the comfort of her niece, Pollyanna, were complete.

In the kitchen, Nancy sent her flat iron with a vicious dig across the dish-towel she was ironing.

"'Light hair, red-checked gingham dress, and straw hat'--all she knows, indeed! Well, I'd be ashamed ter own it up, that I would, I would—and her my onliest niece what was a-comin' from 'way across the continent!"

Promptly at twenty minutes to four the next afternoon Timothy and Nancy drove off in the open buggy to meet the expected guest. Timothy was Old Tom's son. It was sometimes said in the town that if Old Tom was Miss Polly's right-hand man, Timothy was her left.

Timothy was a good-natured youth, and a good-looking one, as well. Short as had been Nancy's stay at the house, the two were already good friends. To-day, however, Nancy was too full of her mission to be her usual talkative self; and almost in silence she took the drive to the station and alighted to wait for the train.

1. On what date did the telegram arrive?

    A) 24th June
    B) 25th June
    C) 26th June
    D) 25th July

2. The room contained a bureau. What is a bureau?

    A) A cupboard
    B) A type of window
    C) A bed
    D) A desk

3. Where did Polly go after reading the telegram?

   A) The dining hall
   B) The garret
   C) The garage
   D) The garden

4. Polly was Pollyanna's:

   A) Mother
   B) Niece
   C) Aunt
   D) Cousin

5. What was Polly's reaction to the telegram?

   A) Delighted
   B) Upset
   C) Excited
   D) Reluctant

6. How many centimetres did Polly raise the sash upon killing the fly?

   A) 1cm
   B) 2.5cm
   C) 2cm
   D) 5cm

7. What shapes make up Pollyanna's dress pattern?

    A) Squares

    B) Triangles

    C) Circles

    D) Pentagons

8. Who was Nancy?

    A) Pollyanna's sister

    B) Polly's staff-member

    C) Polly's sister

    D) Polly's cousin

9. Who was old Tom?

    A) Timothy's brother

    B) Timothy's son

    C) Nancy's son

    D) Timothy's father

Answer Sheet: Comprehension 7

Mark your answers with a pencil like this:

[A]

1	[A]	[B]	[C]	[D]
2	[A]	[B]	[C]	[D]
3	[A]	[B]	[C]	[D]
4	[A]	[B]	[C]	[D]
5	[A]	[B]	[C]	[D]
6	[A]	[B]	[C]	[D]
7	[A]	[B]	[C]	[D]
8	[A]	[B]	[C]	[D]
9	[A]	[B]	[C]	[D]

Mark: ☐ / 9

Comprehension 8: St Paul's Cathedral

St Paul's Cathedral is one of the largest churches in the world. It is located within the City of London on Ludgate Hill, the City's highest point. The cathedral was designed by Sir Christopher Wren, as an important part of a huge rebuilding plan, after the Great Fire of London in 1666. Wren also designed over 50 other London churches.

St Paul's Cathedral was the tallest building in London from its construction until 1962. The dome is the second largest in the world at 366 feet high and is reached by climbing 259 steps.

The present cathedral was built between 1675 and 1710, although other church buildings have stood on the same spot. Old St Paul's Cathedral was started by the Normans and completed by about 1240.

One of the most well-known features of the cathedral is the Whispering Gallery. A whisper against the wall can be clearly heard at the other side, 112 feet away.

The cathedral's crypt is the largest in Western Europe and extends the entire length of the building. There are over 200 monuments and memorials in the crypt.

The cathedral was hit by several German bombs during the Blitz in World War Two. One was removed before it exploded; had it done so, it would have totally destroyed St. Paul's.

The designer of the new cathedral was the first person to be buried there. The cathedral's largest monument is that to the Duke of Wellington, depicting the Duke riding a horse.

Funeral services for several famous people have been held at St Paul's, including Winston Churchill and Lord Nelson. The matrimony of Prince Charles and Princess Diana was also held there.

St Paul's Cathedral has been painted by such famous artists as Pissarro, Canaletto and Turner. It has also been shown in several films, including *Mary Poppins*, *Sherlock Holmes* and one of the *Harry Potter* films.

1. Where is the City's highest point?

    A) Sir Wren's house
    B) City of London centre
    C) Ludgate Hill
    D) St Paul's hill

2. Why was the Cathedral being built again?

    A) Due to the Great Fire of London
    B) It was being made bigger
    C) It was being relocated
    D) It was destroyed by a German bomb in the WW2

3. Who started the first St Paul's Cathedral?

    A) Sir Robert Wren
    B) A group of religious members
    C) The Normans
    D) Sir Christopher Wren

4. Which of the following statements is true?

    A) St. Paul's Cathedral is the tallest in the world
    B) The dome is the second largest in the world
    C) The dome can be reached by climbing 343 steps
    D) The most recent Cathedral was built by the Normans

5. In the whispering gallery, how many centimetres (approx.) away can a whisper be heard?

    A) 112cm
    B) 3360cm
    C) 336cm
    D) 456cm

6. Which of the following statements is true?

    A) The crypt is the largest in Europe
    B) There are over 500 monuments in the crypt
    C) The crypt is the largest in Western Europe
    D) The crypt is the largest in the world

7. Who was the first person to be buried in St Paul's Cathedral?

    A) Sir Christopher Wren
    B) A Norman person
    C) Duke of Wellington
    D) It is unclear

8. Whose royal wedding was held at St. Paul's?

    A) Sir Christopher Wren and his wife
    B) Prince William and Prince Kate
    C) Queen Elizabeth and Prince Philip
    D) Prince Charles and Princess Diana

9. Which of the following statements is true?

   A) The Cathedral was shown in 3 Harry Potter films.
   B) Winston Churchill's funeral was held there.
   C) The Cathedral has never been shown in a film.
   D) Winston Churchill was born there.

Answer Sheet: Comprehension 8

Mark your answers with a pencil like this:
   [A]

1	[A]	[B]	[C]	[D]
2	[A]	[B]	[C]	[D]
3	[A]	[B]	[C]	[D]
4	[A]	[B]	[C]	[D]
5	[A]	[B]	[C]	[D]
6	[A]	[B]	[C]	[D]
7	[A]	[B]	[C]	[D]
8	[A]	[B]	[C]	[D]
9	[A]	[B]	[C]	[D]

Mark: ⬜ / 9

Answers

Comprehension 1

1	B
2	C
3	A
4	B
5	B
6	A
7	B
8	D
9	A

Comprehension 2

1	D
2	B
3	A
4	B
5	A
6	C
7	A
8	C
9	A

Comprehension 3

1	B
2	A
3	D
4	C
5	B
6	B
7	D
8	A
9	C

Comprehension 4

1	D
2	C
3	B
4	D
5	C
6	A
7	C
8	A
9	A

Comprehension 5

1	A
2	C
3	B
4	B
5	B
6	C
7	C
8	D
9	A
10	B

Comprehension 6

1	B
2	C
3	A
4	D
5	B
6	D
7	A
8	B
9	C

Comprehension 7

1 A
2 D
3 B
4 C
5 D
6 B
7 A
8 B
9 D

Comprehension 8

1 C
2 A
3 C
4 B
5 B
6 C
7 A
8 D
9 B

Printed in Great Britain
by Amazon